God's Little Instruction Book
for Leaders

Honor Books
Tulsa, Oklahoma

4th Printing

God's Little Instruction Book for Leaders
ISBN 1-56292-622-5
Copyright © 1999 by Honor Books
P.O. Box 55388
Tulsa, Oklahoma 74155

INTRODUCTION

What makes a great leader? Some people believe leaders are *born,* and others are just as sure that leaders are made. Some use the terms *manager* and *leader* interchangeably, while others would debate that one title has nothing to do with the other. Still others would say that the person with *control* is the leader. What do you believe?

Harry Truman once said, "Men make history and not the other way around. In periods where there is no leadership, society stands still. Progress occurs when courageous, skillful leaders seize the opportunity to change things for the better."

We at Honor Books believe Godly leaders are people of principle, integrity, and self-control, more interested in serving others than themselves. Leaders are people of action. They motivate others, yet they are never afraid to take responsibility. Are you a leader?

In *God's Little Instruction Book for Leaders,* we are proud to offer you a collection of time-honored quotations and Scriptures to encourage, inspire, and motivate you to be the best leader you can be. Let them encourage you to fulfill your dreams!

Wisdom is the wealth of a great leader.

Blessed is the man who finds wisdom, the man
who gains understanding, for she is more profitable
than silver and yields better returns than gold.

Proverbs 3:13-14 NIV

$\mathbb{A}$ great man is always
willing to serve others.

★★★

But the greatest among you shall be your servant.
Matthew 23:11 NAS

Never, never, never … give up.

And let us not grow weary while doing good, for in
due season we shall reap if we do not lose heart.
Galatians 6:9 NKJV

To love what you do and feel that it matters—how could anything be more fun?

★ ★ ★

When you eat the labor of your hands, You shall be happy, and it shall be well with you.
Psalm 128:2 NKJV

The test of a first-rate work
is that you finish it.

★★★

I have fought a good fight, I have finished my course.
2 Timothy 4:7

Dreams don't work unless you do.

The desire of the sluggard puts him to death,
for his hands refuse to work.
Proverbs 21:25 NAS

Clear your mind of *can't.*

★★★

I can do all things through Christ who strengthens me.
Philippians 4:13 NKJV

Trust men and they will be true to you; treat them gently and they will show themselves great.

Two are better than one, because they have a good return for their work: If one falls down, his friend can help him up.

Ecclesiastes 4:9-10 NIV

11

Life is a coin. You can spend it any way you wish, but you can only spend it once.

For what is your life? It is even a vapor that appears for a little time and then vanishes away.

James 4:14 NKJV

Diligence is the mother of good fortune.

★★★

The hand of the diligent makes rich.
Proverbs 10:4 NKJV

$\mathbb{L}$ord, grant that I may always desire
more than I can accomplish.

★★★

Forgetting what lies behind and reaching forward to what lies ahead.
Philippians 3:13 NAS

The secret of success is to do the common things uncommonly well.

Do you see a man skilled in his work? He will serve before kings; he will not serve before obscure men.
Proverbs 22:29 NIV

Efficiency is doing things right.
Effectiveness is doing the right thing.

★★★

Do what is right and good in the sight of
the Lord, so that it may go well with you.
Deuteronomy 6:18 NRSV

16

$\mathbb{A}$ statue has never been set up in honor of a critic.

★★★

Let us not therefore judge one another.
Romans 14:13

Don't equate activity with efficiency.

★★★

Let all things be done decently and in order.
1 Corinthians 14:40

Laughter adds richness, texture, and color to otherwise ordinary days.

A happy heart makes the face cheerful,
but heartache crushes the spirit.
Proverbs 15:13 NIV

$\mathcal{Y}$ou can accomplish more in one hour with God than in one lifetime without Him.

Walk in wisdom ... redeeming the time.
Colossians 4:5

The way to get to the top is to get off your bottom.

The soul of a lazy man desires, and has nothing;
But the soul of the diligent shall be made rich.

Proverbs 13:4 NKJV

An honest man's word is
as good as his bond.

★★★

Let your "Yes" be "Yes," and your "No," "No."
James 5:12 NKJV

Laziness travels so slowly that poverty soon overtakes him.

★★★

Yet a little sleep, a little slumber, a little folding of the hands to sleep:
So shall thy poverty come as one that travelleth;
and thy want as an armed man.

Proverbs 24:33-34

In the long run, men hit only what they aim at.

★★★

Therefore I do not run uncertainly (without definite aim).
1 Corinthians 9:26 AMP

24

$\mathbb{E}$nthusiasm is contagious.
It's difficult to remain neutral
or indifferent in the presence
of a positive thinker.

★★★

Finally, brethren, whatever is true ... honorable ... right ... pure ...
lovely ... of good repute, if there is any excellence and if
anything worthy of praise, dwell on these things.
Philippians 4:8 NAS

25

Find out what you love to do,
and you will never have to
work another day in your life.

Stand at the crossroads and look; ask for the ancient paths, ask where
the good way is, and walk in it, and you will find rest for your souls.
Jeremiah 6:16 NIV

Experience is not what happens to a man; it's what a man does with what happens to him.

For whatever is born of God overcomes the world; and this is the victory that has overcome the world—our faith.

1 John 5:4 NAS

The person who knows "how" will always have a job. The person who knows "why" will always be his boss.

How much better to get wisdom than gold! And to get understanding is to be chosen rather than silver.
Proverbs 16:16 NKJV

$\mathbb{D}$evelop the hunter's attitude ...
wherever you go, there are ideas
waiting to be discovered.

For everyone who keeps on asking receives; and
he who keeps on seeking finds; and to him who
keeps on knocking, [the door] will be opened.

Matthew 7:8 AMP

29

Take first things first.
That process often reduces the
most complex human problems
into manageable proportions.

★★★

But seek ye first the kingdom of God, and his righteousness;
and all these things shall be added unto you.
Matthew 6:33

Courage is resistance to fear,
mastery of fear—not
the absence of fear.

★★★

Therefore take up the full armor of God, so that you
may be able to resist in the evil day, and having
done everything, to stand firm. Stand firm therefore.

Ephesians 6:13-14 NAS

The business of finding fault
is very easy, and that of
doing better is difficult.

Therefore you have no excuse, everyone of you who passes judgment,
for in that which you judge another, you condemn yourself;
for you who judge practice the same things.

Romans 2:1 NAS

Remember the difference between a boss and a leader: a boss says "Go!"—a leader says "Let's go!"

Let us go up at once, and possess it; for we are well able to overcome it.
Numbers 13:30

Some people succeed because they are destined to, but most people succeed because they are determined to.

Work hard and become a leader; be lazy and never succeed.
Proverbs 12:24 TLB

34

He who has a *why* to live can bear almost any *how*.

★★★

Never forget your promises to me your servant, for
they are my only hope. They give me strength in
all my troubles; how they refresh and revive me!

Psalm 119:49-50 TLB

Nothing is particularly hard if you divide it into small jobs.

He [Abram] divided his forces against them by night, he and his servants, and defeated them, and pursued them.

Genesis 14:15 NAS

It is the character of very few men to honor without envy a friend who has prospered.

A friend loves at all times.
Proverbs 17:17 NRSV

$\mathbb{A}$ man who does not read good
books has no advantage over
the man who *can't* read them.

Apply thine heart unto instruction, and
thine ears to the words of knowledge.
Proverbs 23:12

38

Life can't give me joy and peace; it's up to me to will it. Life just gives me time and space; it's up to me to fill it.

I have set before you life and death, the blessings and the curses; therefore choose life, that you and your descendants may live.

Deuteronomy 30:19 AMP

Never allow your sense of self to become associated with your sense of job. If your job vanishes, your self doesn't.

★★★

What advantage does man have in all his work
which he does under the sun? A generation goes and
a generation comes, but the earth remains forever.

Ecclesiastes 1:3-4 NAS

Men, for the sake of getting a living, forget to live.

★★★

Every man should eat and drink, and enjoy
the good of all his labour, it is the gift of God.
Ecclesiastes 3:13

41

The art of being wise is the art of knowing what to overlook.

★★★

A man's wisdom gives him patience;
it is to his glory to overlook an offense.
Proverbs 19:11 NIV

Remind me each day that the race is not always to the swift and that there is more to life than increasing its speed.

Now every athlete who goes into training conducts himself temperately and restricts himself in all things. They do it to win a wreath that will soon wither, but we [do it to receive a crown of eternal blessedness] that cannot wither.

1 Corinthians 9:25 AMP

He that has learned to obey
will know how to command.

★★★

And the LORD shall make thee the head, and not the tail; and thou
shalt be above only, and thou shalt not be beneath; if that thou
hearken unto the commandments of the LORD thy God, which
I command thee this day, to observe and to do them.

Deuteronomy 28:13

He who would be a good
leader must be prepared
to deny himself much.

Then said Jesus unto his disciples, If any man will come after me,
let him deny himself, and take up his cross, and follow me.

Matthew 16:24

There is no failure except
in no longer trying.

Be strong, courageous, and firm; fear not ... for it is the Lord your God
Who goes with you; He will not fail you or forsake you.

Deuteronomy 31:6 AMP

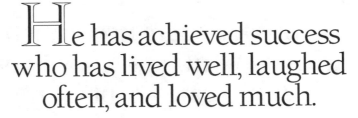

He has achieved success
who has lived well, laughed
often, and loved much.

★★★

Go then, eat your bread in happiness and drink your wine
with a cheerful heart; for God has already approved your works.

Ecclesiastes 9:7 NAS

People don't care how much
you know until they know how
much you care about them.

And though I have the gift of prophecy, and understand all mysteries,
and all knowledge; and though I have all faith, so that I could
remove mountains, and have not charity, I am nothing.

1 Corinthians 13:2

If you can't face the music, you'll never get to lead the band.

Young man, do not resent it when God chastens and corrects you, for his punishment is proof of his love. Just as a father punishes a son he delights in to make him better, so the Lord corrects you.

Proverbs 3:11-12 TLB

The size of your success is
determined by the size of your belief.

Everything is possible for him who believes.
Mark 9:23 NIV

Be great in the little things.

He who is faithful in a very little thing is faithful also in much; and he who is unrighteous in a very little thing is unrighteous also in much.
Luke 16:10 NAS

Opportunities are seldom labeled.

★★★

As we have therefore opportunity, let us do good unto all men,
especially unto them who are of the household of faith.
Galatians 6:10

Many a man has found
the acquisition of wealth only
a change, not an end, of miseries.

He who loves money will not be satisfied with money, nor
he who loves abundance with its income. This too is vanity.
Ecclesiastes 5:10 NAS

I am defeated, and know it, if I meet any human being from whom I find myself unable to learn anything.

A wise man will hear, and will increase learning; and a man of understanding shall attain unto wise counsels.

Proverbs 1:5

Success seems to be largely a matter of hanging on after others have let go.

Let us hold fast the confession of our hope
without wavering, for He who promised is faithful.
Hebrews 10:23 NKJV

If you keep saying that things are going to be bad, you have a chance of being a prophet.

Thou art snared with the words of thy mouth,
thou art taken with the words of thy mouth.

Proverbs 6:2

$\mathbb{A}$ great deal of good can be done in the world if one is not too careful who gets the credit.

So then, whether you eat or drink, or whatever you may do, do all for the honor and glory of God.

1 Corinthians 10:31 AMP

Show me a man who cannot bother to do little things, and I'll show you a man who cannot be trusted to do big things.

You have been faithful and trustworthy
over a little; I will put you in charge of much.
Matthew 25:21 AMP

58

Faith is daring the soul to go
beyond what the eyes can see.

Now faith is the substance of things
hoped for, the evidence of things not seen.

Hebrews 11:1 NKJV

Good words are worth much and cost little.

Pleasant words are a honeycomb,
sweet to the soul and healing to the bones.
Proverbs 16:24 NAS

I don't know the secret to success, but the key to failure is to try to please everyone.

No one can serve two masters; for either he will hate the one and love the other, or he will hold to one and despise the other.
Matthew 6:24

It is a mistake to look too far ahead. Only one link of the chain of destiny can be handled at a time.

★★★

So do not worry about tomorrow; for tomorrow will care for itself. Each day has enough trouble of its own.
Matthew 6:34 NAS

Iʼt's the job that's never started that takes the longest to finish.

★★★

The way of the sluggard is blocked with thorns,
but the path of the upright is a highway.
Proverbs 15:19 NIV

Let not thy will roar when thy power can but whisper.

★★★

A gentle tongue [with its healing power] is a tree of life,
but willful contrariness in it breaks down the spirit.

Proverbs 15:4 AMP

The world is full of willing people:
some willing to work,
the rest willing to let them.

Then He said to His disciples, "The harvest
is plentiful, but the workers are few."
Matthew 9:37 NAS

65

The most difficult secret for a man to keep is the opinion he has of himself.

I warn everyone among you ... not to have an exaggerated opinion of his own importance, but to rate his ability with sober judgment.

Romans 12:3 AMP

Νo one ever said on their deathbed:
I wish I would have spent
more time at work!

★★★

Then I considered all that my hands had done and the toil I had spent
in doing it, and again, all was vanity and a chasing after wind.

Ecclesiastes 2:11 NRSV

No one is useless in this world who lightens the burden of anyone else.

Bear ye one another's burdens, and so fulfill the law of Christ.
Galatians 6:2

68

Do not follow where the path may lead—go instead where there is no path and leave a trail.

Your ears shall hear a word behind you, saying, "This is the way, walk in it."
Isaiah 30:21 NKJV

There is one thing alone that stands the brunt of life throughout its length: a quiet conscience.

If our hearts do not condemn us, we have confidence before God.
1 John 3:21 NIV

70

My obligation is to do the right thing. The rest is in God's hands.

If you know that he is righteous, you may be sure
that every one who does right is born of him.
1 John 2:29 RSV

When you soar like an eagle, you attract hunters.

Be of sober spirit, be on the alert. Your adversary, the devil,
prowls around like a roaring lion, seeking someone to devour.
1 Peter 5:8 NAS

Do not condemn your neighbor;
you do not know what you
would have done in his place.

Do not judge, or you too will be judged. For in the
same way you judge others, you will be judged.
Matthew 7:1-2 NIV

Every Christian needs half an hour
of prayer each day, except when
he is busy. Then he needs an hour.

Evening and morning and at noon will I pray,
and cry aloud, And He shall hear my voice.
Psalm 55:17 NKJV

74

Expect great things *from* God. Attempt great things *for* God.

★★★

Truly, truly, I say to you, he who believes in Me,
the works that I do, he will do also; and greater works
than these he will do; because I go to the Father.

John 14:12 NAS

Never follow the crowd if you want the crowd to follow you.

Follow what is altogether just (uncompromisingly righteous),
that you may live and inherit the land which your God gives you.

Deuteronomy 16:20 AMP

Anybody can do their best.
God helps us to do better
than our best.

★★★

Now glory be to God who by his mighty power at work within us is
able to do far more than we would ever dare to ask or even dream of.

Ephesians 3:20 TLB

Shallow men believe in luck ...
strong men believe in cause and effect.

Be not deceived; God is not mocked: for whatsoever
a man soweth, that shall he also reap.

Galatians 6:7

Dost thou love life? Then do not squander time, for that is the stuff life is made of.

★★★

Remember how short my time is.
Psalm 89:47

79

Don't let your learning
lead to knowledge, let your
learning lead to action.

But be ye doers of the word, and not hearers only,
deceiving your own selves.
James 1:22

Procrastination is the thief of time.

He also that is slothful in his work is
brother to him that is a great waster.
Proverbs 18:9

It is never wise to underestimate an enemy. We look upon the enemy of our souls as a conquered foe; so he is, but only to God, not to us.

For we wrestle not against flesh and blood.
Ephesians 6:12

82

Never play not to lose; always play to win.

★★★

But thanks be to God, Who gives us the victory
[making us conquerors] through our Lord Jesus Christ.
1 Corinthians 15:57 AMP

Saddle your dreams before you ride 'em.

Write the vision, and make it plain upon tables,
that he may run that readeth it.
Habakkuk 2:2

You do not lead by hitting people over the head—that's assault, not leadership.

And the servant of the Lord must not strive;
but be gentle unto all men, apt to teach, patient.
2 Timothy 2:24

$\mathbb{A}$n inconvenience is only an adventure wrongly considered.

For the gate is small and the way is narrow
that leads to life, and there are few who find it.
Matthew 7:14 NAS

Destiny is not a matter of chance; it is a matter of choice. It is not a thing to be waited for; it is a thing to be achieved.

I press toward the goal for the prize of
the upward call of God in Christ Jesus.
Philippians 3:14 NKJV

Imagination was given to man to compensate him for what he is not. A sense of humor was provided to console him for what he is.

A merry heart doeth good like a medicine.
Proverbs 17:22

Far and away the best prize that life offers is the chance to work hard at work worth doing.

Wealth obtained by fraud dwindles, but the one who gathers by labor increases it.

Proverbs 13:11 NAS

Do not persist in folly.
It is not a badge of character to
continue down the wrong road.

The way of a fool is right in his own eyes,
But he who heeds counsel is wise.
Proverbs 12:15 NKJV

Man cannot discover new oceans
unless he has the courage to
lose sight of the shore.

★★★

Now the just shall live by faith: but if any man
draw back, my soul shall have no pleasure in him.
Hebrews 10:38

Plant your feet on solid ground, and you will flourish as a leader of men.

The [uncompromisingly] righteous shall flourish like the palm tree [be long-lived, stately, upright, useful, and fruitful]; they shall grow like a cedar in Lebanon [majestic, stable, durable, and incorruptible].

Psalm 92:12 AMP

Patience and diligence, like faith, remove mountains.

"Have faith in God," Jesus answered. "I tell you the truth, if anyone says to this mountain, 'Go, throw yourself into the sea,' and does not doubt in his heart but believes that what he says will happen, it will be done for him."

Mark 11:22-23 NIV

I think the one lesson I have learned
is that there is no substitute
for paying attention.

Like an earring … of gold or an ornament of fine gold
is a wise reprover to an ear that listens and obeys.
Proverbs 25:12 AMP

94

When we do the best that we can,
we never know what miracle
is wrought in our life, or
the life of another.

And whatever you do, do it heartily, as to the Lord and not to men.

Colossians 3:23 NKJV

It is better to wear out than to rust out.

★★★

Whatever your hand finds to do, do it with all your might.
Ecclesiastes 9:10 NIV

Nothing will ever be attempted
if all possible objects must
first be overcome.

The sluggard says, "There is a lion in the road!
A lion is in the open square!"
Proverbs 26:13 NAS

He who conquers others is strong.
He who conquers himself is mighty.

He who is slow to anger is better than the mighty,
And he who rules his spirit than he who takes a city.
Proverbs 16:32 NKJV

Wisdom outweighs any wealth.

She [wisdom] is more precious than rubies;
nothing you desire can compare with her.
Proverbs 3:15 NIV

$\mathbb{W}$hat counts is not the number
of hours you put in, but how
much you put in the hours.

Therefore be careful how you walk, not as unwise men, but as wise,
making the most of your time, because the days are evil.
Ephesians 5:15-16 NAS

100

The way for a young man to rise is to improve himself every way he can.

Buy the truth and sell it not; not only that, but also get discernment and judgment, instruction and understanding.
Proverbs 23:23 AMP

Wise men are not always silent, but they know when to be.

★★★

There is a time for everything, and a season for every activity
under heaven: . . . a time to be silent and a time to speak.
Ecclesiastes 3:1,7 NIV

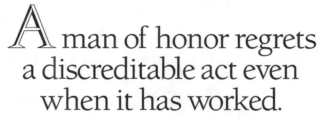

A man of honor regrets
a discreditable act even
when it has worked.

★★★

A wise man's heart directs him toward the right, but
the foolish man's heart directs him toward the left.

Ecclesiastes 10:2 NAS

103

None will improve your lot, if you yourselves do not.

Study to shew thyself approved unto God.
2 Timothy 2:15

Whether you think you can or you can't, you are right.

For as he thinketh in his heart, so is he.
Proverbs 23:7

I is impossible to rightly govern the world without God and the Bible.

Do you see a man wise in his own eyes?
There is more hope for a fool than for him.

Proverbs 26:12 NAS

$\mathbb{B}$egin to act boldly. The moment one definitely commits oneself, heaven moves in his behalf.

Let us therefore come boldly unto the throne of grace, that we may obtain mercy, and find grace to help in time of need.
Hebrews 4:16

Waste no more time arguing what a good man should be. Be one.

Be an example (pattern) for the believers in speech,
in conduct, in love, in faith, and in purity.
1 Timothy 4:12 AMP

Take calculated risks. That is
quite different from being rash.

★★★

The plans of the diligent lead to profit
as surely as haste leads to poverty.
Proverbs 21:5 NIV

Eagles don't flock. You have to find them one at a time.

★★★

Stand therefore [hold your ground], having tightened the belt of truth around your loins and having put on the breastplate of integrity and of moral rectitude and right standing with God.

Ephesians 6:14 AMP

Talk low, talk slow, and
don't say too much.

Do not be hasty in word or impulsive in thought
to bring up a matter in the presence of God.
Ecclesiastes 5:2 NAS

Indecision is often worse than the wrong action.

★★★

A double minded man is unstable in all his ways.
James 1:8

It is better to take a risk now
than always to live in fear.

★★★

The Lord is my helper, and I will not fear what man shall do unto me.
Hebrews 13:6

He who bestows his goods upon the poor shall have as much again, and ten times more.

★★★

If you give to the poor, your needs will be supplied!
Proverbs 28:27 TLB

Genius is divine perseverance.

★★★

Fear not; stand still (firm, confident, undismayed) and see
the salvation of the Lord which He will work for you today.

Exodus 14:13 AMP

Endurance is not just the ability
to bear a hard thing, but
to turn it into glory.

★★★

Do not, therefore, fling away your fearless confidence,
for it carries a great and glorious compensation of reward.
For you have need of steadfast patience and endurance, so that
you may perform and fully accomplish the will of God.
Hebrews 10:35-36 AMP

I use not only all the brains I have,
but all I can borrow.

★★★

For the LORD gives wisdom, and from his mouth
come knowledge and understanding.
Proverbs 2:6 NIV

Protect your own credibility. One of
the highest accolades is the comment,
"If he says so, you can bank on it."

Righteous lips are the delight of kings;
and they love him that speaketh right.
Proverbs 16:13

The quest for excellence is
a mark of maturity.
The quest for power is childish.

★★★

Daniel was preferred above the presidents and princes,
because an excellent spirit was in him; and the king
thought to set him over the whole realm.

Daniel 6:3

The grass may look greener on the other side, but it still has to be mowed.

Be content with such things as ye have.
Hebrews 13:5

120

Identify your highest skill and devote your time to performing it.

★★★

Wherefore the rather, brethren, give diligence to make your calling
and election sure: for if ye do these things, ye shall never fall.
2 Peter 1:10

No man ever became wise by chance.

★★★

The wise have eyes in their head, but fools walk in darkness.
Ecclesiastes 2:14 NRSV

Millions saw the apple fall, but Newton was the one who asked *why*.

Get wisdom: and with all thy getting get understanding.
Proverbs 4:7

Every job is a self-portrait of the person who does it. Autograph your work with excellence.

Many … have done well, But you excel them all.
Proverbs 31:29 NKJV

He who has learned to obey will know how to command.

★★★

Obey me, and I will be your God and you will be my people.
Walk in all the ways I command you, that it may go well with you.
Jeremiah 7:23 NIV

The man who is born with a talent
which he is meant to use finds
his greatest happiness in using it.

But life is worth nothing unless I use it for doing
the work assigned me by the Lord Jesus.
Acts 20:24 TLB

Learn the luxury of doing good.

★★★

Do not withhold good from those who
deserve it, when it is in your power to act.
Proverbs 3:27 NIV

$\mathbb{A}$ man is not finished
when he is defeated.
He is finished when he quits.

Fight the good fight of faith.
1 Timothy 6:12

One of the marks of
true greatness is the ability
to develop greatness in others.

Teach these great truths to trustworthy men
who will, in turn, pass them on to others.
2 Timothy 2:2 TLB

Genius is 1 percent inspiration and 99 percent perspiration.

For just as the body without the spirit is dead,
so also faith without works is dead.

James 2:26 NAS

We make a living by what we get—we make a life by what we give.

It is more blessed to give than to receive.
Acts 20:35 NAS

Honesty is the cornerstone of all success, without which confidence and ability to perform shall cease to exist.

Let me be weighed on honest scales, That God may know my integrity.
Job 31:6 NKJV

The words of a leader can motivate men to scale the highest mountain or fight for justice and freedom against tyranny.

Death and life are in the power of the tongue.
Proverbs 18:21 NKJV

$\mathbb{A}$ll I have seen teaches me to trust the Creator for all I have not seen.

Trust in the LORD with all your heart,
And lean not on your own understanding.
Proverbs 3:5 NKJV

Most of the things worth doing
in the world had been declared
impossible before they were done.

With men this is impossible; but with God all things are possible.
Matthew 19:26

In life, as in football,
you won't go far unless you
know where the goalposts are.

Where there is no vision, the people perish.
Proverbs 29:18

In the race to be better or best, don't forget to enjoy the journey!

★★★

Be happy ... and rejoice and be glad-hearted continually (always).
1 Thessalonians 5:16 AMP

I t's one of the hardest things in the world to accept criticism … and turn it to your advantage.

★★★

Now no chastening seems to be joyful for the present, but painful; nevertheless, afterward it yields the peaceable fruit of righteousness to those who have been trained by it.

Hebrews 12:11 NKJV

Here is a piece of advice that is worth a king's crown: To hold your head up, hold your overhead down.

Any enterprise is built by wise planning,
becomes strong through common sense, and
profits wonderfully by keeping abreast of the facts.
Proverbs 24:3-4 TLB

Good thoughts bear good fruit;
bad thoughts bear bad fruit—
and man is his own gardener.

★★★

We demolish arguments and every pretension that sets itself up
against the knowledge of God, and we take captive
every thought to make it obedient to Christ.

2 Corinthians 10:5 NIV

Give me a stock clerk *with* a goal, and I will give you a man who will make history. Give me a man *without* a goal, and I will give you a stock clerk.

Fixing our eyes on Jesus ... who for the joy set before Him endured the cross ... and has sat down at the right hand of the throne of God.

Hebrews 12:2 NAS

Great minds have purpose; others have wishes.

★★★

"For I know the plans I have for you," declares the LORD,
"plans to prosper you ... to give you hope and a future."
Jeremiah 29:11 NIV

A wise man will make more opportunity than he finds.

A man's gift maketh room for him, and bringeth him before great men.
Proverbs 18:16

$\mathbb{M}$ake every decision as if you owned the whole company.

★★★

He that handleth a matter wisely shall find good.
Proverbs 16:20

He who considers his work beneath him will be above doing it well.

All a man's ways seem innocent to him,
but motives are weighed by the LORD.
Proverbs 16:2 NIV

$\mathcal{S}$uccess is the result of working hard, playing hard, and keeping your mouth shut.

Even a fool is thought to be wise when he is silent.
It pays him to keep his mouth shut.
Proverbs 17:28 TLB

Self-control is the ability to keep cool while someone is making it hot for you.

A soft answer turns away wrath, but grievous words stir up anger.
Proverbs 15:1 AMP

I would rather walk with God in the dark than go alone in the light.

Even when walking through the dark valley of death I will not be afraid, for you are close beside me, guarding, guiding all the way.

Psalm 23:4 TLB

You must have long-range goals to keep you from being frustrated by short-range failures.

For the vision is yet for an appointed time....
Though it tarries, wait for it; Because it will surely come.
Habakkuk 2:3 NKJV

It takes more to plow a field than merely turning it over in your mind.

Faith by itself, if it is not accompanied by action, is dead.

James 2:17 NIV

150

True contentment is the power
of getting out of any situation
all that there is in it.

I have learned the secret of being content in any and every situation.
Philippians 4:12 NIV

People may doubt what you say, but they will believe what you do.

My little children, let us not love in word,
neither in tongue; but in deed and in truth.
1 John 3:18

Leaders are ordinary people with extraordinary determination.

★★★

Let us run with patient endurance and steady and active persistence
the appointed course of the race that is set before us.

Hebrews 12:1 AMP

The difference between ordinary and extraordinary is that little "extra."

In a race, everyone runs but only one person gets first prize. So run your race to win.
1 Corinthians 9:24 TLB

$\mathbb{A}$ll our dreams can come true—
if we have the courage
to pursue them.

Be strong and courageous, and act; do not fear nor
be dismayed, for the Lord God, my God, is with you.
1 Chronicles 28:20 NAS

He who would climb the ladder must begin at the bottom.

★★★

Anyone wanting to be a leader among you must be your servant.
And if you want to be right at the top, you must serve like a slave.
Matthew 20:26-27 TLB

I make progress by having people around me who are smarter than I am—and listening to them.

Blessed (happy, fortunate, to be envied) is the man who listens to me, watching daily at my gates, waiting at the posts of my doors.

Proverbs 8:34 AMP

ACKNOWLEDGMENTS

We acknowledge and thank the following people for the quotes used in this book: Winston Churchill (6,62), Katherine Graham (7), Arnold Bennett (8), Peter J. Daniels (9), Samuel Johnson (10,73,97), Ralph Waldo Emerson (11,20,75,134), Lillian Dickson (12), Cervantes (13,21), Michelangelo (14), John D. Rockefeller Jr. (15), Zig Ziglar (16,46), Jean Sibelius (17), Harvey Mackay (18), Tim Hansel (19), Dr. Eugene Swearingen (21), Johann Wolfgang von Goethe (22,45,121), Benjamin Franklin (23,79), Dennis Waitley (24,124), Friedrich Wilhelm Nietzsche (25,34), James Huxley (26), Diane Ravitch (27), Roger von Oech (28), Dwight D. Eisenhower (29,81), Mark Twain (30,37), St. Francis de Sales (31,71), E. M. Kelly (32), Henry Ford (34,100), Aeschylus (36), Gordon van Sauter (38), Margaret Fuller (39), William James (40), Edward Gibson (41), Solon Bale (42), O. L. Crain (43), Elbert Hubbard (44,101), David J. Schwartz (48), John A. Shedd (50), Lucius Annaeus Seneca (51,122), George Herbert Palmer (52), William Feather (53), Isaac Singer (54), Lawrence D. Bell (56), George Herbert (57), Bill Cosby (58), J. R. R. Tolkien (60), Robert Frost (62), Marcel Pagnol (63), Sir Thomas Fuller (64), Charles Dickens (65), Euripides (66), Martin Luther King Jr. (68), Milton S. Gould (69), William Carey (72), Catherine Booth (74), Edward Young (77), Sam Snead (78), David Mahoney (79), Mary Webb (80), G. K. Chesterton (81,146), Oswald Chambers (82), William Jennings Bryan (83), Horace Walphole (84), Theodore Roosevelt (85,91), Baltasar Gracian (86), Ronald E. Osborn (88), Diane Sawyer (89), Helen Keller (90), William Penn (93), Michael Aspen (94), Bishop Richard Cumberland (96), H. L. Mencken (98), Sophocles (99), Marcus Aurelius (103), George S. Patton (104), Thomas Alva Edison (105), George Washington (106), Gerald R. Ford (107), Thomas Fuller (108), Horace (109), William Danforth (111), George P. Burnham (112), James L. Hayes (113), John Bunyan (114), William Barclay (116), Woodrow Wilson (117), Barbara Baruch (118), Max Lucado (119), B. C. Forbes (120), Richard Nixon (123), Solon (125), Oliver Goldsmith (127), J. C. Macaulay (129), Louis D. Brandels (130), Arnold Glasgow (131), Lawrence Scott (133), Conrad Hilton (135), J. C. Penney (136), Washington Irving (137), Francis Bacon (138), Robert Townsend (139), James Allen (140), James Cash Penney (141), Edward John Phelps (142), Mary Gardiner Brainard (143), Charles C. Noble (144), Walt Disney (150), Harry J. Kaiser (157).

Additional copies of this book and other titles are
available from your local bookstore.

God's Little Instruction Book
God's Little Instruction Book II
God's Little Instruction Book III
Leadership 101 by John C. Maxwell
The Heart of a Leader by Ken Blanchard

If you have enjoyed this book, or if it has
impacted your life, we would like to hear from you.
Please contact us at:

Honor Books
Department E
P.O. Box 55388
Tulsa, Oklahoma 74137
Or by e-mail at info@honorbooks.com